THE LAST MATCH

BY ANNA ZIEGLER

DRAMATISTS
PLAY SERVICE
INC.

THE LAST MATCH
Copyright © 2018, Anna Ziegler

All Rights Reserved

SPECIAL NOTE

SPECIAL NOTE ON SONGS AND RECORDINGS

THE LAST MATCH had its world premiere at the Old Globe Theatre in San Diego, California (Barry Edelstein, Artistic Director; Michael G. Murphy, Managing Director) on February 13, 2016. It was directed by Gaye Taylor Upchurch, the set design was by Tim Mackabee, the costume design was by Denitsa Bliznakova, the lighting design was by Bradley King, the sound design was by Bray Poor, and the production stage manager was Diana Moser. The cast was as follows:

TIM	Patrick J. Adams
SERGEI	Alex Mickiewicz
MALLORY	Troian Bellisario
GALINA	Natalia Payne

THE LAST MATCH was originally produced in New York City by Roundabout Theatre Company (Todd Haimes, Artistic Director; Julia C. Levy, Executive Director; Sydney Beers, General Manager) at the Harold and Miriam Steinberg Center for Theatre/Laura Pels Theatre on October 24, 2017. It was directed by Gaye Taylor Upchurch, the set design was by Tim Mackabee, the costume design was by Montana Blanco, the lighting design was by Bradley King, the sound design was by Bray Poor, and the production stage manager was Samantha Watson. The cast was as follows:

TIM	Wilson Bethel
SERGEI	Alex Mickiewicz
MALLORY	Zoë Winters
GALINA	Natalia Payne

A workshop production of THE LAST MATCH was presented at New York Stage and Film & Vassar at Powerhouse Theater in July 2015. It was directed by Gaye Taylor Upchurch. The cast was as follows:

TIM	Lorenzo Pisoni
SERGEI	Alex Mickiewicz
MALLORY	Pascale Armand
GALINA	Natalia Payne

CHARACTERS

TIM—mid-30s, a professional tennis player. An all-American golden boy. Effortlessly charming. Faux-humble. Polite in a Midwestern kind of way, with a façade that's difficult to crack.

SERGEI—mid-20s, a Russian professional tennis player. He's fiery, funny, sarcastic, with a short fuse. Whatever he feels, he feels deeply. A lover and a hater, in extremes. A wounded soul.

MALLORY—mid-30s, Tim's wife and a former player. She's tough and spunky and driven, with a mischievous streak and a joyful temperament. Easily frustrated by anything remotely irritating.

GALINA—mid/late 20s, Sergei's girlfriend, also Russian. The definition of no-nonsense; she's hot-tempered and means business. She is also devoted and serious, loveable and loving, in her way.

NOTE

The play is made up of scenes inside a tennis match and memories that take place outside of it. As much as possible, transitions from one to the other should seamlessly blur these boundaries, so that, for instance, the line of dialogue that serves as the bridge from one kind of scene to the other feels that it applies to both worlds.

When I want something—that to me is not youth exactly, but the opposite of death. That to me is a way to always feel like I am nowhere near the end.

—Heidi Julavits, *The Folded Clock*

Let me put it another way: when I am with my son I feel the bracing speed of the one-way journey that guides human experience.

—Sarah Manguso, *Ongoingness*

The slow-motion euthanasia that time inflicts on athletic talent is, for me, the hardest thing to watch in sports. But time is treating Federer with a tenderness that almost defies reason.

—Brian Phillips, "The Sun Never Sets:
On Roger Federer, Endings, and Wimbledon"

The first time you win, nobody picks you; the last time you win, nobody picks you... You've just got to pick yourself.

—Venus Williams

How strange the way success and failure contained each other. How close vindication and humiliation had proved.

—Allegra Goodman, *Intuition*

The long day wanes; the slow moon climbs; the deep
Moans round with many voices. Come, my friends,
'Tis not too late to seek a newer world.
Push off, and sitting well in order smite
The sounding furrows; for my purpose holds
To sail beyond the sunset, and the baths
Of all the western stars, until I die.
It may be that the gulfs will wash us down;
It may be we shall touch the Happy Isles,
And see the great Achilles, whom we knew.
Though much is taken, much abides; and though
We are not now that strength which in old days
Moved earth and heaven, that which we are, we are,
One equal temper of heroic hearts,
Made weak by time and fate, but strong in will
To strive, to seek, to find, and not to yield.

—Tennyson, "Ulysses"

THE LAST MATCH

Lights up on Sergei and Tim, who face the audience. Tim is mid-30s, wholesome, Midwestern; Sergei is in his mid-20s and speaks with a thick Russian accent. They're both professional tennis players at the top of the game.
We begin at love all.

TIM. It's not exactly a whizzing sound—

SERGEI. No, it's more of a whoosh. Like a "whoosh" right past your ear—

TIM. I'd say it's fast and it's slow all at once.

SERGEI. Yeah, it's "sh-sh-sh-sh-sh"—and you are forgetting for a second that everyone is there and it's just FUCK. You think "Sergei, you asshole." You don't understand why you are not good enough.

TIM. No. For me, it was always, you know, credit to him for getting it past me.

SERGEI. *(Rolling his eyes, sarcastic.)* Oh yes, for me too. Absolutely. Credit to him.

TIM. And when *you* hit one, I mean, when you hit an ace yourself, you are…well, you are intensely *alive* in that moment.

SERGEI. *(Taunting him.)* How nice that must feel, to be so intensely alive.

TIM. *(Taking the high ground.)* From the very first point, the match was close.

SERGEI. In those kinds of matches, there is tension all the way through. It never breaks. You are tired just from that, even more than from the physical exertions.

TIM. It had rained and now there was this eerie light when we came out on court.

SERGEI. A late start. All day I sat and then stood and then sat and then stood, shaking out my legs. That's what you do. You try to rest without staying still.

TIM. The press in New York was…the media was into it.

SERGEI. It had been leaked—Tim Porter will retire after this US Open.
What did I think? I don't know. This is sport. You play your game. It does not matter what people say.

TIM. Really, Sergei?

SERGEI. *(A sharp shift.)* Hey, for all I know, you leaked this rumor yourself. To get in my head so I do not give my all in first ever US Open semifinal. Like announcing you will die but really wanting to live and taking a very Russian-like manipulating approach to staying alive.

TIM. I didn't leak the rumor because it wasn't true.

SERGEI. Yes, that is the thing… Even with his up and down playing, even though he is old OLD man at thirty-four years of age, he is still Tim Porter, the favorite in any match he plays. You cannot imagine he will ever go away.

TIM. It's the US Open. I've played it twelve times. Made ten semifinals. Nine finals. Won six of 'em.

SERGEI. *(Sarcastic.)* And I have ten fingers and ten toes. I keep track of things very carefully too.

TIM. *(Taunting Sergei.)* I was *gonna* say if you'd told me when I was a kid that I'd hold that trophy over my head six times, I'd have said you were the biggest liar there was.

SERGEI. But this year, how many trophies have you won?

>   *Tim shoots him a dirty look.*

Lose in Australia, second round; lose in France, quarterfinals. Wimbledon—what a loss! First round, to a qualifier, an eighteen-year-old from Galveston, Texas whose life will never be as good as it was that night. Yes, in last year, it has been lose lose lose.

TIM. *(With a smile, ribbing him.)* And yet…I'm still ranked in the top five and you have yet to crack the top ten, even though as a junior you were being heralded as the second coming of Christ… or of me, or something.

SERGEI. And so people talk. He must be done for, they say. The end of Tim Porter… And they want that. And also they don't want it at all.

TIM. We start the warm up.

SERGEI. Already I am hot hot hot. Like burning up hot. I can feel every tingle in every tingly spot in my body.

TIM. This is Sergei for you. Really no more than a boy.

SERGEI. No, Tim Porter, I have not felt like boy since I was five-years-old child.

TIM. Whatever you say, buddy.

SERGEI. See, we are always a little on edge with each other.
Me and Tim Porter.
Not really friends.

TIM. We practice our serves. Throw the ball up, slam the racquet down. It's a motion I could do in my sleep.

SERGEI. Why don't you take it easy, Tim? You're not young anymore.

TIM. Goad all you want. I've made it through five rounds without dropping a set.

SERGEI. So have I.

TIM. This is my tournament—my house. I own this court; I always have and I will again. I have to. I have to…because my son is here. He's two months old. And it feels like the sky's a different color than it's ever been before.

SERGEI. Tim is very sentimental about this little boy.

TIM. After a long line of—"This has Tim's last final written all over it," and, "We might never see Tim this deep in the second week of a slam again"—it changes here. No more losing.

SERGEI. *(Getting really worked up by the end.)* No more walking off court embarrassed to be seen by anyone, especially the people you love. No more hatred for all the players ahead of you, who create such jealousy in you that you are ashamed to know yourself. To shake their hands in front of the cameras, to make nice, to smile, when really you are wishing so many bad things happen to them.

TIM. And we're only in the warm up.

SERGEI. *(An aside, to the audience.)* And yet. In the "He is done for," in the "This is the end of Tim Porter," is the end of all of us, yes?

TIM. I hate to break it to you, Sergeyev, but I'm not going anywhere.

SERGEI. I hate to break it to *you*, Tim Porter, but we're all going to the same place.

TIM. We starting, or what??

SERGEI. Yeah. I want to start.
I'm ready for you. Tim Porter.

TIM. Are you sure?

> *A scoreboard lights up: Set #1.*

SERGEI. He got the toss and elected to serve.

TIM. You choose to serve first no matter what. It's a psychological thing. Right, Sergei?

SERGEI. They are chanting his name: "Porter, Porter, Porter"— and he wins first game pretty easily… Or another way of looking at it is I lose first game pretty easily.

> *Scoreboard: T. Porter, 1–0*

TIM. I take the first game so fast and in that moment you don't feel the pressure and the failure and the death and the ambition and the coming up short. It's one of those. When you feel like you can do anything. Like you're eighteen years old, with everything in front of you.

> *Mallory enters; they are mid-conversation.*

MALLORY. *(Teasing him.)* You wish you were eighteen.

TIM. This is four years ago.

MALLORY. You wish you were eighteen and that your body didn't make creaking noises and that people weren't calling you old on TV.

TIM. This is Mallory.

MALLORY. But, you know, happy birthday.

TIM. Gosh, thanks honey.

MALLORY. The good thing is: I will love you when you're actually old. When no one talks about you on TV anymore. When they can't even remember your name.

TIM. Where's my present?

MALLORY. What present?

TIM. What do you mean "what present"?

MALLORY. Isn't it enough that all the guys on tour are celebrating today? There are parties happening all over the world. *Tim Porter turns thirty*. He's gotta start showing his age soon.

TIM. *(Matter-of-fact.)* So I'm ready for that present now.

MALLORY. I mean, I know you've been, like, winning slams and stuff, but I've been pretty busy lately too.

TIM. I hope Angie knows how lucky she is. That girl won the lottery with you. You're gonna be a kickass coach.

MALLORY. *(Laughing.)* Well, she's nineteen. At nineteen, you don't think about luck. You just *know* your life is gonna go exactly as planned.

TIM. She's gonna be the biggest star. And it's gonna be because of you.

> Beat.

MALLORY. So…do you remember when you proposed to me?

> *He stares at her, suspicious.*

TIM. Okay, what are you up to.

MALLORY. Nothing. Do you remember or not?

TIM. *(Teasing her.)* …wait. I know it'll come to me.

MALLORY. I certainly hope you'd remember the best day of your life.

TIM. Well…a close second to winning Wimbledon for the first time—

MALLORY. *(Smiling.)* You *are* an asshole, you know that?

TIM. No no, I think I've got it. We were at that weirdo's wedding…

MALLORY. Inga's not that weird.

TIM. Okay, she's *objectively* weird, but it doesn't matter. She's up there *singing* her vows and I believe I took your hand. Really tenderly, *really* romantically. And it was incredibly damp.

MALLORY. That is a load of BS, Tim Porter, and you know it.

TIM. And then later in the night, I took you into the hallway—

MALLORY. Right next to the *bathrooms*—

TIM. I wanted it to be picturesque.

MALLORY. And you asked if I could feel it too.

TIM. Well, I didn't say it quite like that.

MALLORY. "Do you feel it too?" That's what you said. And I looked at you. And your face was so open, and so kind. And I did. Feel it. So I said, "What if I do?"

TIM. And I said: "Well—if you do—I think we should get married."

MALLORY. I was overwhelmed.

TIM. No, you were *silent* and I didn't know what to do, and suddenly heard myself saying…"Can you dig it?"

MALLORY. And I said yes.

TIM. And it was all I could do not to say I told you so because you were such a pain when I first asked you out. But I realized it wasn't the right moment for that sorta thing. Not the right note for that particular melody.

MALLORY. Happy birthday, Timmy.

She hands him a wrapped gift.

TIM. See, I knew you got me something.

He opens the gift and pulls out a pair of plain white socks.

MALLORY. You don't like them?

TIM. *(Lying, and not very well.)* No. I love them. Thank you, honey.

She starts to walk away, but then turns back.

MALLORY. *(Totally offhand.)* Oh, and we're having a baby.

TIM. What?

MALLORY. *(Now living the emotion of it.)* We're having a baby.

TIM. *(To the audience.)* It's the most beautiful melody in the world. And for that moment you don't feel the pressure and the failure and the death and the ambition and the coming up short.

MALLORY. *(A bit teary.)* Can *you* dig it?

TIM. I can dig it.

He takes her in his arms and kisses her. Then she exits.

(To the audience, sadly.) That was the first pregnancy.

SERGEI. We're between games. We switch sides of the court. I pass Tim and even though he has won first game he looks as though he has lost it. I wonder if he is trying to "psych" me out, but I will not let him.

TIM. Then a woman in the crowd calls out—

SERGEI. This idiot camel just screams out: "We love you, Tim Porter!!" And I must tune this out. Tune it out, Sergei. You do not need their love. But the camel keeps yelling: "Don't go, Timmy, please don't go!"

TIM. Go where? I wanna say. Outside of here what would I do everyday? What would that even look like?

SERGEI. Oh don't worry. Not much will change. You'll still be same gigantic asshole. Trust me.

TIM. I'm not an asshole.

SERGEI. You don't want people to *know* you're an asshole. But anyone who does this sport at this level is gigantic asshole of worst gigantic asshole variety.

TIM. I net an easy return.

SERGEI. You have to care only for yourself.

TIM. I barely manage a lob and then it lands long anyway.

SERGEI. You cannot have anything but want.

TIM. Sergei slams a volley into my face and it's all I can do to get my racquet up to protect myself.

SERGEI. I take my time. Sometimes, even though the ball is moving at such incredible speeds, you can take your time. And I did.

TIM. Three points played, three points lost. Fuck me.

SERGEI. And then I get a little confident, just a little, and I run to the net and boom—he passes me.

TIM. I'm not an asshole.

SERGEI. One shot here—another point.

TIM. I care about my family.

SERGEI. One shot there—another point.

TIM. I love my son. All my want is want for him.

SERGEI. Really, Tim Porter? *All* your want?

TIM. And suddenly it's deuce.

SERGEI. And then it is deuce again. And again. And again.

TIM. *Fourteen* deuces.

TIM and SERGEI. Fourteen.

SERGEI. On and on and on. And the voice in my ear that is saying, "Take this. Just take it. It is yours. Fuck you," turns into my darling Galina's voice. Her actual voice:

GALINA. *(Like the volume's been cranked up as loud as it can go.)* TAKE IT SERGEI!! TAKE IT NOW!

SERGEI. And I know I will be in deep trouble if I do not hold this game—even more trouble than I will be in with myself. But I can't help it—in most important matches the thought that…*I cannot win*…won't go away.

> *Galina enters.*

GALINA. No, Sergei—when you start to think you undo yourself. Thinking is not your strength. Hitting a ball over a net at great speeds and with impressive precision—that is your strength.

SERGEI. *(With a smile, pride.)* Galina—she does not mince the words.

GALINA. Why should I not say what I mean? Why talk if you do not get your point across? Furthermore, this Tim Porter—he is beaten down. He is a little little man right now. His heart will not be in it, and you will capitalize.

SERGEI. And I say to her: His heart does not need to be in it as long as his racquet is. And she screams at me. It is right before the match and Galina and I are fighting. Okay yes. We are always fighting. So this was like always.

GALINA. No, you idiot! Don't let up on him. Not even once. Don't let him get under your skin. Once you do that, you're finished.

SERGEI. He is already under my skin—he was number one player for three years running! He is legend. His name is written on the fucking sky.

GALINA. Well, you will be legend. You will be one soon enough. If you do your job.

SERGEI. Why don't you go out there and play him if you're sure it's so simple.

GALINA. Oh, you sound like my mother: "Why don't you go to work and earn the money if you insist on buying that fancy lipstick. No girl your age needs lipstick, let alone a fancy one like that, plus it make you look like whore." So I say "My lips are my lips, to do with as I please" and she say "I made those lips" and I say "I am not inside of you and have not been inside of you for many years during which time I have come to see how everything about you is despicable" and she say "You are awful terrible child, I don't believe I *did* make you" and then she retreat into her little hole where she always went and we did not speak for weeks and eventually I grew up, moved out of the house and found you who will go be brave in ways she could not.

SERGEI. So in other words there is no pressure on me.

GALINA. Sergei!

SERGEI. Galina!

GALINA. I am not joking around.

SERGEI. No, you never are.

GALINA. When I met you, I knew, right away, that you were a champion.

SERGEI. Did you.

GALINA. I said to Natasha, "This one will make something of himself. I know it because there are things he prefers to do than spend time with me." See, in the past, my many boyfriends always put me first, above all other things. But not you. And I was so happy.

TIM. The fifteenth deuce. And the crowd is going bananas. You just want to please them, your parents times a million.

SERGEI. No, the crowd is not my parents. My parents are my parents…

GALINA. Don't think of that now.

SERGEI. I know, but.

GALINA. Don't be scared to win. To beat him!

SERGEI. I'm not.

GALINA. You are. He is too big. This icon of your growing up. You have put an impossible pressure on yourself and it frightens you.

SERGEI. I'm not scared!!

GALINA. *(Smiling, mission accomplished; and giving him a little pat on the behind.)* Okay, okay.

SERGEI. *(Back to the audience.)* Yes, I was. I was very scared.

TIM. The sixteenth deuce, and I could really feel the whole stadium just pulling for me.

SERGEI. I try to focus on the fans. And they are really pulling for me. There are not so many Russians here but the good thing about Russians is that they are very loud.

TIM. The next day, the journalists wrote about that moment, when the crowd got to their feet. When all I could think was: "Remember this, Tim. Remember this."

SERGEI. It had never happened before like this for me. As though you are sun and everyone else is planets and stars and moons. It is, as they say, *intoxicating*, as though you have taken very strong drug like crack or cocaine, which I have only tried on handful of occasions so I cannot really comment.

TIM. I had the advantage more at the beginning but he always got out from under me. Then, somewhere in the middle, he starts winning the deuce points and I start having to grind it out.

SERGEI. So many game points, on my racquet. This should be MY game so many times over. I have earned it! But life does not actually work that way. You actually have to win.

TIM. And that's when the rumor comes back into my mind. My retirement… My retirement. And all of a sudden I can't breathe. I mean, I can't even breathe.

SERGEI. He hits a second serve return into the net, straight into the net, and so I take it. After all those deuces, I win the game. Second game of match but it feels like I have won whole thing. Wham bam thank you, ma'am! Sergei takes it.

GALINA. Oh yes he does!

  Scoreboard: 1–1

TIM. *(A stupid question.)* Was it demoralizing?

SERGEI. Galina was in my box, just going crazy.

GALINA. *(Translation: "Kill the bastard.")* Ubey ublyudka, / Seryozha!!

SERGEI. She is happy but still looks as though she might kill some-one. And that is Galina at her most contained.

TIM. And then I'm just, I don't know, one game after the next—2–1, 3–1, 4–1—they're seeping out, like milk gushing out of the carton onto the kitchen floor.

SERGEI. Suddenly I'm up 5–1 and serving for the set! This is not what anyone predicted. Not even Galina predicted this. She thought I'd be fighting my tooth and my nail for every point, the whole way through.

TIM. So yeah. I lose the game, and I lose the first set.

GALINA. Yes!!

SERGEI. If I were text message, I would be exclamation point exclamation point question mark exclamation point emoji of face of an obese sixty-year-old man who has been very badly backed up for days and has just taken biggest shit of his life.

TIM. Yeah. It was demoralizing.

> *First set: Sergeyev 6–1. The lights shift. Mallory is exercising to a video—rigorous and fast-paced. She's pushing herself incredibly hard. She's entirely focused. Tim is watching but she doesn't know he's there; then suddenly she sees him out of the corner of her eye and jumps.*

MALLORY. Jesus, how long have you been standing there?!

TIM. Don't stop on my account.

> *She turns off the video.*

MALLORY. Don't watch me, Tim. It's creepy.

TIM. Sorry…
I thought you looked good…

MALLORY. *(With a wry smile.)* Then you might need to get your eyes checked.

TIM. You were going pretty hard there.

MALLORY. *(Pumped up; this is the solution she's been looking for.)* I just started thinking maybe I shouldn't be making Angie do things I can't do myself, you know?

TIM. Oh yeah?

MALLORY. So from now on I'm gonna just show her how it's done. No more excuses. I can't stand her whining.

TIM. *(With a note of skepticism.)* All right.

MALLORY. What?

TIM. It's just that I thought half the fun of coaching was *not* having to do that stuff. Not having to stay in that kind of shape.

MALLORY. Coaching isn't supposed to be fun. It's a job.

TIM. No, I just meant—

MALLORY. If I don't kill her first, that is. Do you know what she said to me today? She was like, "Yeah, I heard that after thirty-five, a woman's chances of having a healthy baby go WAY down." I wanted to slap her.

TIM. Maybe you should have.

MALLORY. Right?! I mean a nineteen-year-old has no concept of—

TIM. You don't have to work with her anymore… I mean, you don't have to work at all.

She shoots him a look.

MALLORY. Come on, Timmy.

TIM. What?

MALLORY. You know I can't just be Tim Porter's wife.

TIM. Yeah it's hard to imagine a fate more dreadful.

MALLORY. The vessel that carried Tim Porter's children. What was her name again?

TIM. *(Teasing her.)* I don't know but man was she pretty.

MALLORY. *(Playfully slapping him.)* The first time I sat in the stands to watch you, I came home to find stuff online about Tim Porter's / "sweaty new girlfriend."

TIM. *(With a smile, ribbing her.)* Sweaty new girlfriend.

MALLORY. I mean, *I'd just played a match!* A second-round match in the *French Open*. And won by the way. But still there I was, just a sweaty girlfriend.

TIM. Not to me.

MALLORY. I mean, what if having a baby is just boring?

TIM. Okay we're talking about babies now??

MALLORY. And some people don't even love their babies right away so it's just relentless and boring. And we already have tennis for that, right?

TIM. Well, I don't find tennis boring.

MALLORY. I know. It's shocking.

TIM. Mallory.

MALLORY. Being a father would distract you.

TIM. I'm not gonna play forever.

MALLORY. But deep inside you really think you will.

TIM. No I don't.

MALLORY. I did.
I mean, there's *still* some part of me that thinks I'll go back one day. That I'm not really done.

TIM. Don't you want to be done?

MALLORY. *(Matter-of-fact.)* Well, I always completely hated it.

TIM. Yeah you did.

MALLORY. But at least I knew why I was here, what I was supposed to do every day. I had all this…clarity. In some ways it didn't even matter that I was a failure.

TIM. You weren't a failure.

MALLORY. *You* can't say that to me, honey.

TIM. You were one of the top twenty players in the whole world.

MALLORY. Uh-huh. And would that have been good enough for *you*?

    Beat.

Exactly. So I can't fail now. I'm gonna make her a star. Angie. *(With a wry smile.)* Even if she is an asshole.

TIM. …You know you haven't let me down, right? Is that what this is about?

    Beat.

MALLORY. I'd be nearly six months pregnant now. Have you

thought about that?

Tim doesn't say anything.

Because I think about it every day.

She exits.

TIM. That was the second pregnancy.

SERGEI. I have all the momentum going into the second set. This is good thing, yes, but you can't get too cozy-cozy. You always must play as if you are the one behind.

TIM. My dad once said to me, "You love it, right?" meaning tennis, and I was like yeah, sure, of course I love it. What do you mean, do I love it? It's air for me; it's how I breathe.

Scoreboard: Set #1, S. Sergeyev 6–1; Set #2, 0–0

SERGEI. At start of second set, Tim is concentrating less and less. It is like he has decided he will lose and is simply watching it happen. I go up 1 – love.

TIM. But over the years, yeah…I guess I started wondering if, really, I was just good at it, you know?

SERGEI. 2 – love. And the life has gone out of the crowd. You don't want to watch a man get slaughtered so you call your wife; you get hot dog; you check stock market on your cell phone—"Oh jeez, my stock is down."

TIM. A few years back, my dad had a minor thing. A minor heart attack, I guess, so not such a big deal, but…

SERGEI. Everything is going my way; I see ball so clearly, as though it is huge, like melon, and also a part of me, my hand, my fingers…

TIM. He doesn't come to my matches anymore. Made him too tense and the doctors didn't like it. But now I look up at my box and my dad isn't there. My dad…who for years ran five miles before breakfast but now wears hearing aids and gets winded walking the dog around the block. He put everything in his life on hold for my tennis. I mean, how amazing is that? To do that for your kid? He drove me home after practice every day of my life. We didn't really talk. He'd put on his John Denver or his Neil Diamond and I'd complain but I think we knew we were sitting very deep in the heart of happiness. Back then.

Bang! Sergei hits Tim in the face.

SERGEI. And then I hit him in the face. He is at net and it is not my intention but in the third game of second set, this is what happens.

TIM. He hits me.

SERGEI. / And.

TIM. And I let out this totally—

SERGEI. This loud lady shriek, a scream—

TIM. *(Screaming at Sergei.)* What the hell was that??

SERGEI. I put up my hand in the universal gesture of apology.

TIM. That can't be sincere.

SERGEI. He says:

TIM. You're just gonna stand there?

SERGEI. So I say, "What, you'd prefer I sit?" And the crowd laughs.

   Galina is cracking up.

TIM. That's it. For the past two years, when I've lost more than I've won, at least, at the very least, the crowd has been with me. And my *son* is here. My son is here today. So this was…

SERGEI. He goes crazy.

TIM. *(A humble admission.)* I go a little nuts.

MALLORY. Settle down, Tim. It doesn't matter. Just settle down!

SERGEI. He goes cuckoo. Which for me would be just normal changeover between games, but for Tim is very out of character. Very out of the carefully sculpted character he has built all these years. Not a hair out of place.

TIM. *(Angry and awkwardly delivered.)* I never really liked you— no offense.

SERGEI. No that is not offensive in the least.

TIM. I don't like players like you. Your antics and tantrums and fancy shot-making. I mean, what does it amount to? You've been underperforming your entire career.

SERGEI. I couldn't agree more.

TIM. I mean, who do you think you are??

SERGEI. I am just Sergei Sergeyev, a poor boy from tiny fishing village on Caspian Sea.

TIM. Oh come on. Don't play that humble-beginnings crap with me!

SERGEI. But is true. I did not grow up in Iowa with silver spoon where my dick should be.

TIM. And now you're doing just fine for yourself I'd say. I bet you bought your parents a Porsche last week.

MALLORY. Tim! That's enough.

SERGEI. Actually I gave your mother brand new Porsche after two times fucking her in backseat.

GALINA. *(Watching, her head in her hands.)* Oh, Sergei.

TIM. He really said that. And then Drobek, in the chair, is like "cool it" and Sergei is docked a point.

SERGEI. Me?? *I* am docked the point? It's un-fucking-believable. I mean, yes, I did hit him so hard in face with tennis ball that there is for days afterwards a mark on upper part of his left cheek but that is not against the rules.

TIM. Just because something isn't against the rules doesn't mean you do it!

SERGEI. But I didn't mean to do it!

TIM. You're the best fucking tennis player in the world, don't tell me you didn't mean to do it!

> *A breath.*

SERGEI. *(With real surprise and humility.)* You think I'm the best fucking tennis player in the world?

TIM. You are.

> *Scoreboard: Set #2, S. Sergeyev 2–0.*
> *Sergei is humbled. Galina enters the scene, seamlessly.*

GALINA. *(To an unseen waiter.)* Waiter? Waiter, do you know who this is?

SERGEI. *(He actually loves this.)* Stop it. Galina. You embarrass me.

GALINA. This man will one day be the best tennis player in the entire world. You should pay him the respect of bringing us our wine and some bread within our first twenty minutes of sitting in your supposedly fine establishment, which, might I add, could use a little sprucing up. You are only *two* star Michelin restaurant for a reason, I think. Also I would like to revise my order. Instead I will have the snapper but without the potatoes and without the beurre blanc and please, no garnish of any kind.

SERGEI. So that is basically just piece of fish. That is all you want to eat?

GALINA. No, I want everything in the world. But I also know what I am and am not capable of. I know if I start down a road I will stay on it.

SERGEI. Compulsive? I am this way too, of course.

GALINA. Did you know I was once two hundred pounds, in my childhood?

SERGEI. You were not.

GALINA. I was not. But I felt like I was. Like no one would ever really see me. My mother, she perpetuated this myth and then it became the myth by which I live my life. We all have them, these myths. These fictions, but still they control who we are.
What is yours?

SERGEI. My what?

GALINA. Your myth?

SERGEI. *(Deflecting her question.)* I do not live by myth.

GALINA. You are disagreeing with me?

SERGEI. *(Seeing the error of his ways.)* No. No I am not. I must have myth.

GALINA. What is the thing you want most in the world? ...I for example want to be taken seriously for who I am and not for my body.

SERGEI. Then why do you care so much about your body?

GALINA. Would you be with me if not for my body?

> *Beat.*

SERGEI. No.

GALINA. So I am realistic. I need it to get the things I want. After all, one day you will take me seriously. When you get to know me.

SERGEI. Oh don't worry—I already take you seriously.

GALINA. I was surprised, you know. Your trainer Uly told my cousin Maria that you were a handful. That you had these rages. That you could not be controlled. And then I meet you and you are just this little mouse.

SERGEI. That is because you terrify me.

GALINA. It's true—we are so many different people. This is why I act. It merely emphasizes what is already the case.

SERGEI. You did the commercial for that…plant fertilizer? Uly shows me this on the YouTube. It's funny—that was a wig, yes?

GALINA. I was paid well for that.

SERGEI. So what other parts have you played?

GALINA. Are you making a cross-examination of me, Sergei?

SERGEI. No, I am trying to understand if you are real actor or if it is just dream hobby of yours.

GALINA. How would you like it if I asked if you were real tennis player? What kind of question is this?

SERGEI. I am clearly a real tennis player because I play tennis. All the time.

GALINA. Well, I cannot act whenever I want to—I must be chosen! And this is indignity I do not enjoy and so I do not put myself in the position of facing it very often.

SERGEI. So you are scared.

GALINA. *(Standing to leave.)* Okay. I curse you, and I am leaving because as it turns out you are not at all the kind of person I could ever like or be with!

SERGEI. *(Stopping her from walking out.)* Let me tell you something: Right now I am number fourteen player in the world, yes?

GALINA. So what?

SERGEI. When I went pro, I thought it would be something if one day I could crack top twenty. I thought: That is all I need to be happy in this life.

GALINA. Well, congratulations. You did it.

SERGEI. But that is the thing—I'm not happy. I have to crack top ten. And when I do, I will need to be better than that. It will go on forever.

Even when I am the best fucking tennis player in the world. I am sure of it.

TIM. When I first got number one, I thought: *yes*. I mean, you can't really take it in. *Number one*, right? Fuuuuuck… But the next morning was a gut punch. I woke up sweating, just thinking: How long can I stay here? How can I possibly stay here?

SERGEI. Will you please sit back down.

GALINA. Why?

SERGEI. Because I love you and I want to have dinner with you and have a nice night and to do that you have to sit back down.

> *A beat.*

GALINA. Oh, already you love me, is that right?

SERGEI. …Yeah.

GALINA. Ah. So this is your myth. That love can triumph in the end.

SERGEI. Galina, I am Russian. I do not believe in triumph of love. But I do believe it is possible to have nice meal now and then. Is that too much to ask?

GALINA. For people like us, it might be almost too much to ask.

SERGEI. I bet Tim Porter has nice meal with his wife every single night!

GALINA. But Tim Porter's worst nightmare is probably getting speeding ticket. He was not raised as we were raised. So aware of death.

SERGEI. Okay, this is not conversation that is going to lead to enjoying our meal.

GALINA. Sergei, do you ever feel like, when you are playing tennis in front of all those people, everything else—what you want, what you like, what you fear—drops away? I like to think it feels this way, to play. I cannot have that, but I hope you can.

SERGEI. Why can't you have that?

GALINA. Sergei, I am Russian. I cannot forget the impossibility of happiness.
But you. You are lucky…you can escape who you are.

He looks at her, takes her hand.

SERGEI. Yes: It is very nice when everything else drops away.

TIM. When did we first meet, Sergei?

SERGEI. So I am docked point for claiming to fuck Tim Porter's mother in backseat of car.
And Tim is fired up. And he takes that game.
And he takes the next two games. So he is now up 3–2 in the second set.

TIM. When did we meet?

SERGEI. You are trying to distract me. I'm returning your serve. I'm behind in set. Don't distract me.

TIM. The locker room at Indianapolis?

SERGEI. *(Suddenly exploding.)* The locker room at Indianapolis?? Really?? Really??
(To the audience, an aside.) Of course I remember exactly when I met Tim Porter. It was not in locker room at Indianapolis.

TIM. It was in Atlanta. I'd been hearing about this guy, Sergei Sergeyev. He wasn't going deep in tournaments but he was supposedly this well of untapped potential. So I watched him play. And it was fascinating—you could literally see every thought *as he was having it*—he couldn't hide a thing. Did he play well? No, not in slightest… but I couldn't stop thinking about him, about what it would feel like not to wear any armor.

SERGEI. After my match, we run into Tim. Which is…I mean, *this* is when I meet Tim Porter?? After I embarrass myself so terribly on court? But my coach introduces us. He says, mark his words, I am going to be next Tim Porter.

TIM. *(Sarcastic, downbeat.)* Good luck with that, Sergei.

SERGEI. As though being Tim Porter is so unpleasant. Which surprises me. That he should seem more unhappy than me, even though I am the one who just got miserably beaten by player with no skill, and no style, and no business being out on tennis court.

TIM. Why don't you say how you really feel.

SERGEI. I think you knew where we met. You were just trying to distract me. And it's not gonna work.

TIM. Yes it will. And I pass him down the line—this thing of beauty—and I take the game. 4–2.

SERGEI. No no no no no no no no. Shit. Fuck. Balls.

TIM. He throws his racquet. He jams that thing into the ground and tosses it aside. And then like an animal, he rips his shirt off. Literally tears it off. This is not a good thing. When Sergei gets angry, he gets good, and he knows this as well as anyone.

GALINA. *(With satisfied calm; she knows this is good.)* It is okay to get angry, Sergei. You do what you need to do.

TIM. He takes his service game easily—just so *easily*. I net two returns, completely eff up an overhead, just—"whiff." I mis-timed it.

SERGEI. I ace him. And I won't lie. It's like sex. The best angry-I-will-not-forgive-you sex you have ever had.

TIM. *(To the audience.)* But I can match him. I go there too. The adrenaline kicks in, zero to sixty.

Scoreboard: Set #2, T. Porter 4–3.

SERGEI. Tim serves at 4–3. He answers with two aces—

TIM. Come on!

SERGEI. What a motherfucking camel—and then a serve and volley winner for 40 – love. And then whoosh—another ace—until the call happens.

TIM. A FOOT FAULT?

SERGEI. He contests the call.

TIM. You've gotta be kidding me!

SERGEI. It is, admittedly, a bad call, but of course it is not my place to intervene.

TIM. You can't call a *foot fault* in the semifinals of the US goddamn Open!!

MALLORY. Calm down, Tim. You have to calm down!

TIM. *(Tim's awkward at insults.)* And I never foot fault! I never do it. I say to the line umpire: "You are an awful person, you know that?"

MALLORY. *(Trying to be genuine.)* Good one, Timmy!

SERGEI. He loses point and then he loses game. And then he loses next game, so I am up 5–4.

27

GALINA. You can do it, Sergei. You've got it all—younger legs, stronger serve, longer arms, quicker feet. You are like a bird flying light on the wind compared to him.

SERGEI. And then I am up 40–15 and serving for the second set. Win *one* point and I am up two sets! The match is going according to plan, which is something, really something! But just as I am congratulating myself, I catch glimpse of Tim's box—of his mother holding that little baby and his so anxious wife, and when I look in my box, there is only Galina, and she will be my wife one day but she is not always so nice to me and I know this, I know it, and so I must be playing only for myself and I am not sure, in that moment, if that is enough… And I lose the game.

TIM. *(Pumping himself up.)* Come on!!
Come on.
You got this, Tim. You can do it.

> *The lights shift. Tim looks at Mallory, who sits on a bench, on a practice court, her racquet on her lap. He goes to sit down beside her. He's as smooth as can be.*

TIM. Stacy, right?

MALLORY. What?

TIM. This is ten years ago.

MALLORY. *(Could she have been hearing right?)* What did you call me?

TIM. That's your name—Stacy, am I right?

MALLORY. Um. No.

TIM. Shit. Really?
Well, what is it?

MALLORY. We've, um, we've met before.

TIM. Is that right?

MALLORY. We were juniors…

TIM. No. When?

MALLORY. I'm not gonna tell you that.

TIM. Oh, come on. Throw me a bone.

> *She doesn't say anything.*

Was it at Bollettieri?

MALLORY. I never trained there.

TIM. In Palm Springs?

MALLORY. You really don't remember?

TIM. I meet so many people. You have to forgive me. My brain is just…

MALLORY. *(With a smile, teasing him.)* It's hard to be you, isn't it.

TIM. Come on, be nice.

MALLORY. *(Teasing.)* Okay. I'm sorry. I'm sorry you win every match you play.

TIM. I nearly lost today.

MALLORY. *(Laughing dryly.)* Can I ask you…

TIM. What?

MALLORY. When someone comes that close, is there any part of you that wants to give it to them? Like they deserve it for even getting *close* to beating you?

TIM. Never. You always have to feel like it's yours and they're trying to take it from you. I honestly wouldn't even get on court if I felt there was a chance I was gonna lose.

MALLORY. Wow.

TIM. What?

MALLORY. Maybe you could lend me a little of that? I promise to give it back.

TIM. You've got a match today, don't you?

MALLORY. *(Surprised that he knows this.)* Yeah.

TIM. Petrokova's good. She's got great court coverage. But you'll be fine. Just don't be afraid to exploit her weaknesses. Her forehand return of serve is crappy so hit it there as much as you can. And don't be nervous.

MALLORY. Did I say I was nervous?

TIM. …Do you know what *your* weakness is?

MALLORY. *(Bold, flirty.)* Oh, you know *my* weakness too?

TIM. It's also your strength…

MALLORY. And what's that?

TIM. You anticipate balls so well because you're inside the mind of your opponent. But you're in it too deep. And you start to feel for them.

> *Beat.*

It's a wonderful quality in a person.

MALLORY. *(With a wry smile.)* Maybe not in a tennis player though.

TIM. But who cares about that.

MALLORY. You really don't remember meeting me?

TIM. Wait a second.

MALLORY. What.

TIM. Was it…Rhode Island?

> *She doesn't say anything.*

You won that award?

MALLORY. Which award?

TIM. Was it…Sportsmanship?

MALLORY. I am a very good sport.

TIM. You were that night, with me rambling on and on.

MALLORY. So you do remember.

TIM. Talk about nervous.

MALLORY. Why were you nervous?

TIM. Sitting next to YOU?

MALLORY. Come on, I was sitting next to YOU. And even at sixteen, you were already…

TIM. You were the famous one! The gal who gives out hugs after every match.

MALLORY. I don't understand how anyone *doesn't* do that. You've just been through so much together.

TIM. And there I was thinking a match was about going through so much on your own.

MALLORY. It makes me less nervous to think of it like you're both putting on this show, together.

TIM. Are you nervous right now?

MALLORY. About my match?

TIM. No.

MALLORY. No, I'm not nervous.

TIM. Well I am.

MALLORY. Why?

TIM. Cuz I'm finally gonna get up the nerve to ask you out.

> *Beat.*

MALLORY. Well, I hate to break it to you, but I don't date guys on tour. I don't even really talk to people on tour.

TIM. I know. It's been hard to find you. I've been trying. For, like, ten years.

MALLORY. It's not gonna happen, Tim Porter.

TIM. Okay.

> *He turns as if defeated, then turns back.*

You know…one day we're gonna have children and we're gonna say to them, "Can you believe your mom said no the first time your dad asked her out?"

MALLORY. A minute ago you didn't even know my name.

TIM. I did. I do: Mallory Beth Sinclair.

> *She looks at him in surprise.*

See? I know the whole thing.

SERGEI. He is very wily, Tim Porter. He sneaks up on you like snake. From 5–5, he holds his serve. And then I am serving, at 5–6.
And he passes me on the backhand side with his trademark Tim Porter forehand on a point when I should not have approached the net. He passes me on the forehand side on another point when I should not have approached the net.
It is looking like clinic for kids on passing shot!!
Humiliating.
And then, to make matters worse, at love – 30, I double fault.
I double fault.
To make it triple break point. Triple set point.
All I can say is it is not fun. To be me out on court right now.
Especially when I lose very next point, or rather Tim wins it. He hits winner down the line because *he* is a winner. And I lose. I lose the set.

TIM. The crowd goes crazy. Just absolutely bonkers. "USA, USA," they chant. "Tim Porter for President," someone cries out.

SERGEI. Because if Tim can still play then we're all still young, and…yeah, invincible. And who doesn't want to feel like this?

TIM. I can't help it. I take a bow. I know it's a jerk move, but they're applauding. They love me. How many more times will I have this?

SERGEI. At this moment I cannot stand to look at Tim Porter. Who was once, I admit it…my idol.

GALINA. Sergei, what are you doing?

> *She enters a flashback.*

SERGEI. What?

GALINA. You were falling asleep. At the table.

SERGEI. Was I?

GALINA. I guess you were not fascinated by my cautionary tale of the tennis player my second cousin Vladlena married who had so much potential but left the tour in favor of small apartment in Miami where now Vladlena runs nail salon and he is tennis pro for elderly American Jews.

SERGEI. *(To the audience.)* What I do not say to my Galina is that maybe it is better that this man should have the love of a nice woman in Miami than the dream of playing professional tennis. After all, what are dreams but distractions from something else you have lost?

GALINA. Did you hear me, Sergei? Or are you still asleep??

SERGEI. *(To the audience.)* The night before I had not slept. Maybe one hour. Maybe two. It was that kind of night where you don't know how much you are awake or asleep. This is how most nights were for me.

GALINA. What do you mean you don't get any sleep? How do you play tennis without any sleep?

SERGEI. No, I sleep. Just not great. I don't sleep great.

GALINA. For how long?

SERGEI. Forever.

GALINA. And you never tried to fix it?

SERGEI. You are not sounding sympathetic. I mean, I lie there, staring at ceiling for hours. Every day I am in little bit of hell because I know night will come and I will have to do that ordeal.

GALINA. So what do you think about. As you lie there.

SERGEI. I don't tell people this.

GALINA. We are going back to your house and you will tell me.

SERGEI. My house?

GALINA. Yes.

SERGEI. And so we went. It is difficult to say no to Galina! I had been holding her at arm's length, saying good night at end of dates with kiss on cheek. But I had been wanting this even at the same time as I didn't want it. You have to know that up close, Galina has eyes like stars in sky—bright and dark at once. They are unlike any other eyes I have ever seen.

GALINA. Okay, so tell me.

SERGEI. I don't know.

GALINA. *(She can be a real bully.)* Just tell me!!

SERGEI. Okay! Well… When I was child, I would picture myself hitting ball after ball. And you would think the monotony of this would send one to sleep, but it kept me awake, with the fear that I would miss. You see I was very hard on myself. I had to be. No one—not my parents, not my friends—no one played any sport. But I displayed an extreme skill with hand and eye coordination when I was eleven-months-old baby and when I turned three, my father's friend Mikhael took me to a court and hit with me, and I couldn't get enough. I never wanted to leave.

GALINA. *(Prodding him to get to the point.)* But eventually you did. Because here you are.

SERGEI. At age of nine, I left home. I trained in Italy, and I trained in France, and I trained in America. Always sleeping in bunk beds, smelling other boys' feet. No home. Except for this game. And yet these days, when I cannot sleep, the game is not my home. I see myself hitting balls wildly—no control. I cannot avoid making a mistake. My parents are watching, and I am so embarrassed—I mean *this* is what I left you to do?
To play tennis *badly*?

He looks at her, with need in his eyes.

GALINA. You lost your parents?
I mean…they are gone?

SERGEI. I didn't say that.

GALINA. I know.

SERGEI. They were killed in crash, almost ten years ago. They were on their way to see me play. The flight was delayed, and they called me from the airport. "We might not make it," they said. "Don't be mad."
I was fifteen years old.
I won that match, 7–5, 7–5.
And they weren't there.

GALINA. I am sorry, Sergei.

SERGEI. That was last match of my childhood. That was the last one.

> *Beat.*

GALINA. You know, I too have trouble falling asleep. I never just relax; it always feels there is some way I could help my situation if I could only think of it. This is true from when I was a girl. And maybe this is what got me on plane to America, even though I had no prospects, just cousin with sofa-bed who said, Galina, come here and you can be model; you can be actress, no big deal. There is money falling out of trees if you can only catch it.

SERGEI. So what do you do to get to sleep? When you have trouble?

GALINA. As a child, since my mother was not so much around, my grandma, my babushka, she would put me to sleep. She loved me. I don't know why, but she did. And I would cling to that love, especially I would cling to it at night. Because in sleep you don't know what you will face: your terrible mother or the father you never met. Or worst—you might run into yourself.

SERGEI. I would always love to run into you.

GALINA. *(Quietly, earnestly.)* Thank you.
So I would lay my head on my grandma's lap. She was sharp and bony and brittle but somehow her lap was still soft. And she'd say: "Close your eyes, Galina."

> *Sergei's are still open.*

Close your eyes.

Sergei closes his; he is lying with his head in Galina's lap.

She'd say: "Are they good and closed? No peeking." She'd say: "Now make sure you're in a comfortable position. Think of this position as your home for the night."

And then say to yourself—in your head, in the voice inside yourself— say, "Good night toes." And when you feel your toes go quiet, you will know that they are asleep. Once they are, say, "Good night ankles." Wait for them. Some parts of the body are more stubborn than others. Then, "Good night calves, good night knees." You are working your way up. "Good night thighs, good night tummy."

SERGEI. *(With his eyes closed, whispering.)* I think you missed something.

GALINA. Good night hands. Good night elbows. Good night chin. Good night nose. Good night eyes… Good night day. Good night body… Good night, Sergei. Good night.

> *He is asleep. Beat. The lights shift back to the match. Sergei's eyes are still closed as he sits in his chair; Tim sits at the front of his chair, eager to get going again.*
>
> *Scoreboard: Set #1, S. Sergeyev 6–1. Set #2, T. Porter 7–5. Set #3, 0–0.*
>
> *Sergei finally opens his eyes. We move from silence into action.*

SERGEI. *(Quietly, from sitting.)* It is third set. And the sky is so dark and the lights so bright it seems like almost day.

TIM. I serve first. And now it's a question of music. Of jazz. Of poetry. I mean, you know your favorite song? How sometimes you don't even notice you're singing it? It's like that.

SERGEI. What's your favorite song? "Don't Worry Be Happy"?

TIM. It's been written that Tim Porter in his stride is a better player than any who's ever lived. And no, it wasn't my mother who wrote that. That was the *New York Times*, I believe.

SERGEI. Oh come on—you know precisely it was *New York Times*. You probably know the date.

TIM. *(Can insert more recent date here if need be.)* August fourth, twenty twelve. Chris Clarey.

SERGEI. There are some athletes, they say, whose powers seem more than human. Tim is one of those. In certain moments, it looks like he was born with a racquet in his hand and a purpose. Unlike the rest of us, who must choose who we are and what we do.

TIM. Something happens to my body.

MALLORY. You go Tim. You've got this.

TIM. I'm just flying. And I go up 2–0 in the third set.

SERGEI. I can't do anything about it. It is like I am fourteen again and watching Tim play on tiny television set in my room at the academy.

TIM. I kid you not I know exactly where each ball is gonna go *before* he even hits it. And it feels…

SERGEI. *(A genuine, searching question.)* How *does* it feel?

TIM. *(Humbled.)* It feels…like I will never die.
It feels like I am living precisely the life I was supposed to live.

SERGEI. Wow.

TIM. Yeah.

SERGEI. On the television set, he always wins. And all of the boys at the academy are in awe. If only someday we can be on center court too.

GALINA. You are on center court, Sergei! You have made it! You are here. You deserve this too! *You* are beautiful!

TIM. But it's like Sergei's just…disappeared.

SERGEI. My parents…they didn't want me to play. They thought it was too much. This life. Also they were just humble people, with a little boat. "Why do you need to conquer the world? We don't care if you are something great. You are our boy and we love you."

TIM. He's getting the ball back, but his heart's not in it.

SERGEI. In this set, the third set, while I lose and lose and lose, I am twelve years old. I am home for rare visit and my father and I are out for walk at end of the day. He says to me, "Sergei, race me to that tree over there." And this is surprising because my father does not run—he does not do much that is physical activity. But I am always up for a contest so I take off and he takes off and up until this time I have never beaten my father, not at anything. But I am

36

indeed victorious and I look back and my father is panting and there is a look on his face that is confusing to me; I don't know what to do with it so I say, "Race me to the next tree," and he is too much proud not to so we take off and once again I win. He is panting and holding his knees. And then I say "the next tree" and again we set off. I can't stop. I am so young and so confused and my father is slower with every tree and finally he is on the ground and he says, "No more, Sergei, no more."

GALINA. *(Gently.)* Come on, Sergei, get back in the game.

SERGEI. He did not want me to beat him, and I did not want to beat him but still I did it; I don't know why.

TIM. I am in love with this set. This set is my mom, and my dad when he came to my matches and I would look up at him after every point. It's the first tournament I won as a boy, twelve years old, in Dayton, Ohio, where, when I saw my face reflected in the winner's trophy, I didn't know myself—I was so different from who I'd been even two hours before. This set…is my wife and how easy it was to love her, and it's me as a boy, feeling like I'll be in the world forever. This set has me wrapped in its embrace and it's so warm and so right and I'm playing the best tennis of my life. Of the thirty-four years of my life.

SERGEI. It is in this moment, for first time, that it occurs to me that I want to stop playing tennis.

GALINA. Seryozha, please…

SERGEI. And also that I cannot stop.

Scoreboard: Set #3; T. Porter 5–0.

TIM. I don't feel old, not now. And it actually kinda pisses me off. How good I feel. It makes me wanna clock those numbskulls who think I'm done. I'm not done! Why would anyone stop doing this?

SERGEI. It is my whole life.
On the other hand, I do not enjoy it and it is my whole life. And life is short.

TIM. Sergei blasts one at me, out of nowhere. It lands at my feet, and I pick it up; I scoop gently, the way you field a ball in baseball; I barely touch it; I'm not thinking; I'm just doing, and it's back over the net—the softest, quietest little drop shot you've ever seen.

MALLORY. *(Quietly, in awe.)* You did it. Holy shit you did it, Tim.

TIM. I take the set. Easiest set of my life.

> *The men take a short break.*
>
> *Scoreboard: Set #1, S. Sergeyev 6–1. Set #2, T. Porter 7–5. Set #3; T. Porter 6–0.*
>
> *The fourth set. The men stand again.*

SERGEI. When we stand to start the fourth set, there's a swell in the crowd. The stadium, it starts to rumble. It starts to move.

GALINA. *(Chanting, slowly.)* Sergei. Sergei. Sergei.

TIM. You can feel something shifting.

> *Sergei looks up at Galina, grateful and surprised.*

GALINA. Sergei. Sergei. Sergei.

TIM. She starts chanting his name.

MALLORY. Ignore it, Timmy.

GALINA. Who are you, Sergei? Say your name.

TIM. You've gotta be kidding me. The crowd joins in.

GALINA. Who are you Sergei??

SERGEI. They are chanting *my* name? That cannot be. I cannot be hearing right.

GALINA. Who are you, Sergei? The people, they want to know you! Let them know you!

SERGEI. Who am I? I am orphan from Kaspiysk!

GALINA. Who are you?

SERGEI. I am trapped in body of tennis player who will never get out from under his life.

GALINA. That's not true! You are living your life! This is it! This is your life! Who are you??!!

SERGEI. Sergei! I am Sergei!!!

TIM. It's my own fault. I made it look too easy. Made him too much of an underdog. And they want a match. No one wants to go home.

GALINA. You can do it, my love!!

SERGEI. I can do it! I can do it!!

TIM. It's amazing. How all of a sudden it seems like he's three times the size, covering the court like a giant.

SERGEI. I move through my service game like precision master. One shot here—oh, Tim, you are too slow. One shot there—I'm sorry, Tim, you can't get a racquet on that one.

TIM. Dammit.

SERGEI. It's fun. I am inside of it again and it's fun in here.

MALLORY. Don't let him get to you, Timmy. You're my guy. You can do it. You're our guy.

TIM. And she holds up our son like a trophy and I'm running all over the court, sliding and reaching and grasping.

SERGEI. I'm running you ragged.

TIM. She's holding our son. And I keep thinking: He won't remember this, but also he will. It'll be on the internet for the rest of time. Video of him in the stands, while his dad struggled. Which is exactly what I *wouldn't* want him to see: all of the suffering that goes along with desire.

SERGEI. Not too much left in the tank, maybe, eh?

TIM. *(To Sergei.)* No no, I've got lots left in the tank.
(To audience.) And to prove it, I lunge for a drop shot. I run from behind the baseline up to the net and I lunge and—

SERGEI. And on game point of second game of fourth set—

> *Tim goes down, in intense pain. He tries to get back up, but he can't.*

His back goes out.

TIM. *(Through gritted teeth.)* Shit!

> *We enter a flashback; we weave in and out of it.*

MALLORY. Where does it hurt?

TIM. Shit shit shit.

MALLORY. Timmy?

TIM. It's not a where; it's everywhere. It's everywhere.

MALLORY. This doesn't usually happen in the middle of the night. I mean, it just hit you, just like that? It woke you up?

SERGEI. What people don't realize is how painful it is to try to get well fast. If you are not an athlete, you just let the body heal, slow slow, on its own terms. If you are an athlete…you play through it, which of course makes it even worse.

MALLORY. On a scale from one to ten, what is it.

TIM. I don't know. Eight.

MALLORY. So it's really a ten.

SERGEI. Tim is kneeling down. He is retching on the court, like rabid dog. And everyone just stares. It is, after all, a spectacle. And this is a spectator sport.

> *Mallory kneels down next to Tim, tries to still him, to knead his back, his shoulder; Tim calls out in pain.*

TIM. Aaaaah!

MALLORY. I made it worse?

TIM. Just mix me the drink. Please. Just do the drink.

> *She stands, goes to a table and takes liquids and powders out of her bag.*

MALLORY. I can do that.
But no cortisone shot because we did one a few weeks ago.

TIM. Maybe one of those too.

MALLORY. I can't stand this. I hate to see you this way.

TIM. I would be okay if you just HURRIED THE SLIGHTEST BIT. Could you go any slower, Mallory? God.

MALLORY. I'm going as fast as I can.

TIM. It's just that I'm in fucking agonizing fucking pain.

> *Mallory hands him the drink. Tim sits up and drinks it; the pain abates.*

MALLORY. You've gotta just get the surgery, Tim.

TIM. Not gonna happen.

MALLORY. I don't care if you miss a season.

TIM. Well, I do.

MALLORY. I didn't wanna get my knee fixed but I had to, and so I did it.

TIM. And then you never played again, so.

MALLORY. Okay, I'm gonna go back to bed.

TIM. No—you can't.

MALLORY. I don't like being screamed at in the middle of the night.

TIM. I'm sorry this isn't the most convenient time for you, but I can't exactly control when this happens!!

MALLORY. *(Cutting him off, a weapon.)* I had a miscarriage! Yesterday.

TIM. What?

MALLORY. Yesterday morning. During your match.

TIM. No you didn't.

MALLORY. I didn't wanna tell you this time…but I was nine weeks in.

> *Beat.*

TIM. You shoulda told me, Mal.
You should've told me.

> *She doesn't say anything.*

My god, I don't want you going through this alone.

MALLORY. *(With a rueful smile.)* No way around that, Timmy.

TIM. Well…then maybe we should stop.

MALLORY. What?

TIM. I can't watch you…I can't let you do this to yourself.

MALLORY. Are you crazy? We can't stop now. Not after everything I've…

TIM. I don't want you doing this for me. I can't bear that.

MALLORY. Oh *you* can't bear it?

TIM. I'm sorry, I—

MALLORY. Do you want me to be a failure at everything I set out to do?

TIM. What? No.

MALLORY. It's one thing not to make the top ten in the world; it's another thing not to be able to have a child. I mean, any idiot can have a child. My *parents* could have children.

TIM. I think—understandably—everything feels awful to you at this particular moment. But things usually do work out in the end.

MALLORY. For you, Tim. For you.

TIM. Mallory—

MALLORY. No. We keep going.

SERGEI. Tim takes a time out. He leaves the court. And I wait. It is the longest three minutes of my life.

TIM. *(To the audience.)* I've always thought if a player doesn't wake up in some kinda pain, they're doing something wrong. And that's just the deal. Eleven-month season. No one to sub in for you. It's brutal. You can't add to that worrying about your body ten years down the line. If you did, no one would play at all.

SERGEI. I decide that when he comes back I will not show any mercy.

TIM. There is no place where you are more alone than in your own body.

SERGEI. I have had two operations. My elbow. My hip. I understand this pain, but if you are playing, I will play you, Tim Porter.

TIM. I'm numb all over from the anti-flams. And my back is taped so much I feel like a damn mummy.

SERGEI. He walks back on court very slowly. And oddly tall like he has taken moment to google "good posture."

TIM. Sometimes you need other people to let you know you're okay. And they know you need that. And they give it to you.

SERGEI. There is a roar. And the crowd, it loves him again. He is hurt and he is their golden boy so they must heal him.

TIM. The thing is, your body is *your* body, to do with what you want.

SERGEI. Like the world making room for Tim, once again. And it lifts him up.

TIM. So I'm gonna use it while I still can.

SERGEI. He takes his game. He keeps the points short and hits winner after winner.

TIM. I find some new gear. Full of shortcuts.

SERGEI. It is, frankly, embarrassing to lose to someone so clearly injured. So what do I do? I lose to him *again*. Why not, right? He breaks my serve if you can believe it.

TIM. Heck yeah I do. I tie it right up. 2 all. And then take the next game. I'm in a groove and if I stay in it, I glide right to the finish line.

Scoreboard: Set #4, T. Porter 3–2.

But then without meaning to I glance at my box. And Mallory's head's in her hands. She's not watching. She can't look at me.

SERGEI. Tim? Are you taking another time out, Tim?

TIM. The thing is…when you have trouble having a baby, you walk through the world a little differently. You stare at other people's children. Sometimes you feel your throat closing up, like you can't breathe.
Your parents stop knowing what to say.

I mean, the first time we told them Mal was pregnant, my mom cried. The next day she called and said how all night she'd been remembering when *I* was a baby. That all these things came rushing back to her. Those nights after I was just born.

The second time, they said, "Oh. Well, that's…" They said: "That's wonderful, you two. Truly."

The third time, they said, "Oh really? Gosh. Gosh…"

SERGEI. He cannot stop looking up at box. So I look up too. And my Galina? She is glaring at me. How could I be letting this walking injury defeat me? Many years from now, I remember that look. It will be the look I will see whenever I disappoint her. Which I will do, from time to time. Because that is what happens, in life.

For instance, last year at US Open, I went through three matches like they were nothing. And then in fourth round, I play Bartok who I roomed with at the academy. He has never beaten me, but when we are playing I am remembering how he cried in his sleep for his mother—and he tramples me in this match. And afterwards I am so ashamed. I am walking through the hallways in daze and I do not look up. Until someone says:

TIM. You'll get him next time, Sergei.

SERGEI. *(Awestruck.)* And it is Tim Porter.

TIM. Your head wasn't in it.

43

SERGEI. And I say, "No, my head was nowhere close to that match." And he smiles and says he can count on one hand number of matches where his head stayed in match whole time. And he says my footwork is very—

TIM. You've got some really fancy footwork going there.

SERGEI. And that made me happy, that Tim Porter should take any time out of his day to consider my footwork. And then he walks away. And it occurs to me that he was condescending to me! And that adds injury to insult as you say in America. And so I get frustrated. When will my life be easy?? And that night Galina has gone to bed and I am drinking with Uly and these two ladies come up to us and they are very nice; they say how they love watching me play and I move like Canadian maple syrup what have you what have you. And I am thinking so much my life is unfair—why would Tim Porter say that about my footwork??—that when one of them puts her hand on my dick under the table—she is not shy, I guess—I let her leave it there. And when she suggests we go to her hotel room, yes I go with her. And we fuck so much. And in this time I do not *think about anything*, which feels incredible, even better than the sex we are having.

TIM. Mallory still won't look at me. And now I can feel my back again. It's not a good sign when you're wishing you were still numb. And the problem is: I know what happens now. I know exactly how much pain I'll be in…and I'm afraid, and the fear's even bigger than the pain.

SERGEI. I love my Galina, but sometimes you need to put your foot on the pedal. You need to put your dick where it doesn't belong. This is the nature of want. It takes you crazy places. And it revs you up, like motorboat. I take the next two games, and Tim Porter is left in my wake. 4–3.

Scoreboard: Set #4, S. Sergeyev 4–3.

TIM. I am overwhelmed. It's late December. We're at the doctor's. Mallory is eight months pregnant. Eight. She's been on bed-rest for a month, a month when Angie couldn't spare her, so she let her go, and, well, let's just say that didn't go over well. She's lying on the table—just a routine thing. The doctor's putting that goop all over her belly. She's lubing Mal right up, like an old engine.

MALLORY. *(Not worried, just chatting.)* I haven't felt him moving all that much today, you know.

TIM. The doctor smiled and nodded. Nothing to be worried about.

MALLORY. He's usually such a kicker. He jabs me everywhere. I can't fall asleep he jabs me so much.

TIM. The doctor's smiling and nodding, smiling and nodding. Then she leaves the room, just abruptly. Just like that.

MALLORY. Where'd she go?

TIM. I don't know.

MALLORY. Tim, where'd she go? Why'd she leave like that?

TIM. I don't know.

MALLORY. I don't like that.

TIM. It's fine.

MALLORY. What if it's not fine?

TIM. Don't assume that.

Beat, and now Mallory betrays some worry.

MALLORY. Where'd she go, Tim? Why isn't she coming back??

SERGEI. So I put my foot on the gas! All the wanting, the loss, the work, coming together like car screeching around a curve. It must take fastest route possible to get where it is going but it might crash along the way. It might burn whatever is in its path. I am up 4–3 now, and Tim Porter is what is in my path.

TIM. And then she did come back. And she came back with another, older doctor. And they both listened again for the baby's heartbeat…
And it wasn't there.

MALLORY. What do you mean it's not there? That can't be. I mean, it's there. Maybe he's just sleeping and it's really quiet. Can that happen? Can he just go to sleep?

TIM. Of course they did tests, and of course they waited to tell us, but they knew. I think they knew right away that he was gone.

MALLORY. That's not possible. I walked four miles every day. I drank foul green juice. I made sure I gained enough weight but not too much. I did yoga, kegels. I slept well. I did everything right.

TIM. I didn't know you did all that.

MALLORY. I'm dying, Tim. I'm dying. This is…I can't do it…it's too much.

TIM. They told her she'd have to have the baby. You know, like have it anyway. Go through labor. Better for the body. Safer.

MALLORY. *(Pleading with him and then breaking down.)* You have it. I can't have it. You have it. I can't. I can't. I can't.

SERGEI. I can't stop. I move Tim Porter around court like puppet. He is in pain. But one must take advantage. And I do. I go up 5–3 in fourth set.

TIM. It is silent. It's just…silent when your wife delivers a baby that isn't going to… You hear every sound in a room that feels enormous but still isn't big enough to hold your…I mean, it's just…silent.

SERGEI. Sometimes the ball is cleanly and clearly in and sometimes it just clips tiny fraction of the line. But either way it is in. It is this kind of ball that gets me the set.

GALINA. Incredible, Sergei.

SERGEI. Did you hear that? I win! Fourth set. Where are you, Tim Porter??

> *Scoreboard: Set #4, S. Sergeyev 6–3.*
>
> *Set #5, 0–0.*
>
> *Both men take a break, too unsettled for different reasons even to sit.*

We start the fifth set! And I can tell Tim is in pain.

TIM. All tied up, two sets apiece. But really we're not even.

SERGEI. He is leaning on his racquet between points as though it could support him.

TIM. I feel like I'm going to die on this court.

SERGEI. First to six. That's what we're down to.

TIM. The cortisone is gone. The adrenaline is gone. And the pressure in my back is building, growing, expanding, tighter and tighter.

GALINA. A handful of games. And your life will change.

SERGEI. I am serving for the first game of the set and I hit an ace. An awesome ace. A whoosh.

TIM. I don't even see it; it's that fast.

SERGEI. He is bent over when I serve; he wouldn't have gotten to the ball if I'd hit it right to him. But still—he raises his hand.

TIM. Challenge.

SERGEI. Excuse me?

TIM. I'd like to challenge the call.

SERGEI. A desperation move. But it doesn't matter. They review it and according to their cameras—

TIM. It's out.

SERGEI. What??? One millimeter from the line. And I am: "You've gotta be kidding me." I'm shouting: "Really? Really??!" I am outraged. I don't know where it comes from.

TIM. I assume you're trying to pump yourself up.

SERGEI. I am not trying to do anything. I am out of control. I don't understand how something that felt that good could have been out.

TIM. I look at Drobek. He looks at me. He shrugs. It's like Sergei's *asking* for the point to be taken away. And so he takes it away. Deuce.

SERGEI. No no no no no no. I am sick of things being taken away. Everything in my life is slippery through my fingers. Isn't there anything I can just keep?

GALINA. What do you mean you want to go to a diner?

SERGEI. This is yesterday.

GALINA. I think diners are not very nice. I do not like to use the restroom at such places.

SERGEI. Come on, Lina.

GALINA. And you will ruin your dinner. We are going for such a nice dinner. Don't ruin it.

SERGEI. I will not ruin my dinner. I promise.

GALINA. I will want to get French fries at a diner and then I won't fit into my new dress to wear to dinner tonight.

SERGEI. I would love for you to eat a million French fries but I don't think you will ever eat even one.

GALINA. Why do you want to go so badly to this diner?

SERGEI. I need a grilled cheese sandwich with bacon and a cup of watery chicken soup with those little crackers you crumble inside it. Whenever I am in New York City for United States Open, I have this meal.

GALINA. Well, you have yet to win United States Open so maybe is not such good luck.

SERGEI. Please.

GALINA. Fine, okay. But you will note that it is under duress that I go.

SERGEI. When we get to the diner, I order some French fries. They sit on table untouched.

GALINA. Okay, you have had your grilled cheese with bacon and your watery soup and maybe we can go now? We should rest before dinner. You need to conserve your energy.

SERGEI. What do you think might happen at dinner tonight, Lina?

GALINA. What do you mean by that?

SERGEI. Are you expecting any kind of special event?

GALINA. I am expecting to get annoyed by you a number of times, which would make it not special at all, but quite ordinary.

SERGEI. You don't think I might be taking you out to such a fancy dinner for a purpose?

GALINA. What purpose?

SERGEI. Galina didn't know it, but I had been looking at rings. I had very secretly spoken with diamond dealer. I'd been researching. Cut. Clarity. Grade. At first I said, "I want A-plus-plus diamond!" And they said, no, that is not actually how it works.

GALINA. You're full of shit, Sergei, you know that?

SERGEI. I know you love me, my honey bunny.

GALINA. What of it.

SERGEI. And I love you. Against all my better judgment.

GALINA. Wow, you really know how to flatter a girl.

SERGEI. And so I want you to eat this French fry.

He holds one out to her.

GALINA. But I am not hungry.

SERGEI. I don't care whether or not you are hungry. I want you to eat it because I want to see that the woman I will marry is capable of enjoying this world. Of taking what it has to give.

GALINA. Oh, you will marry me. Is that right?

SERGEI. That's right. And this is no test since I know you will pass it. But the thing is, Galina, my love, this life has a lot of miseries on offer. It is like this diner's menu—

He holds it up.

It is enormous and it is thick with miseries. But occasionally there is daily special. And it is not only made fresh that day, it is good price too! And you have to get it when you see it. You have to buy it and you have to eat it, immediately.

GALINA. This French fry is now standing in for some idea so big I am not sure I understand it.

SERGEI. You are already perfect. Stop working so hard. Relax, for once! What are you hoping to be? You are what I want. And what I will always want, even if you say this is impossible. I believe it is possible. I believe I believe I believe.

GALINA. Hilarious. Sergei.

SERGEI. No, I'm serious.

He gets down on one knee and holds out a ring.

I am asking you, Galina, to marry me.

Beat.

GALINA. Here?!

SERGEI. Here. At this very diner. Isn't it funny and surprising?

GALINA. Do I look like I am laughing??

SERGEI. No, you do not appear to be laughing.

In fact, she is crying. She looks at Sergei, holding out the ring. But instead—she eats a French fry. Slowly. Sergei stands and holds her.

GALINA. I will marry you on the condition that we never go to a diner again.

SERGEI. But we will always go to diners. Now they will be special reminders of our beautiful engagement story.

GALINA. Fuck you, Sergei.

SERGEI. Thank you, my love.

He slides the ring on her finger.

And then we were engaged, and we went to chi-chi restaurant—very fancy—to celebrate, and I was so happy…until I came home to sleep, at which point I could not stop thinking: My parents will never know my wife. And worse: My wife—my children—will never know my parents. It is as though they never existed. They are not here watching most important match of my life, which I am throwing out the window like baby with so much bathwater.

GALINA. Sergei, you must recover from stupid docked point. It is nothing. Move on.

SERGEI. But I am not so good at recovery. Perhaps, when I am docked point, things like this, small small things, it is like reopening wound that has not had chance to heal. And so is painful. And I lose myself in this pain.

Scoreboard: Set #5, T. Porter 2–0.

TIM. I break his serve and then take the second game real quick. I am in so much pain I can't think.

SERGEI. There is something addictive about this pain.

TIM. I just get inside a rhythm and stay there.

SERGEI. There is some way in which you cannot let it go. You hoard it. You keep it like most prized possession.

TIM. Rhythm. That's what it is. When you lose a baby the way we did, and then even though you can't bear it, you make love to try to make another baby, it's rhythm.

MALLORY. I hate you, Tim.

TIM. But it doesn't work. Eventually we try in vitro.

MALLORY. I hate you, Tim, and I regret the day I met you.

TIM. Thanks honey.

MALLORY. My ass is so sore you don't understand.

TIM. I'm sorry.

MALLORY. *(With a smile.)* You should be.

TIM. Mallory.

MALLORY. Yeah.

TIM. I think you're very brave.

SERGEI. It would be very brave to let go of this pain. To live without it holding your hand.

MALLORY. But I don't wanna be brave.

SERGEI. It would mean being responsible for all that you do and all that you are.

MALLORY. This sucks. Just say that this sucks.

TIM. It sucks.

MALLORY. Mean it.

SERGEI. It would mean being alone.

TIM. It sucks!! What do you want me to say? You think I've been having such a great time? No… The pressure to… All the pressure it builds up and all of a sudden my whole body, my back, is…

MALLORY. So it's my fault you have a bad back?

TIM. It's no one's fault. It just is! The pressure is too much. To be "Tim Porter." To stay good at a game that requires so much focus, all the time, and these guys coming up with better bodies, faster—

MALLORY. It's always about the tennis. Isn't it.

TIM. Yes, tennis is a big part of my life. I think you knew that comin' in.

MALLORY. I don't know what I knew. Maybe I just liked you because you were famous and you seemed to like me.

TIM. You can be a real bitch when you wanna be, you know that?

MALLORY. That must put a lot of pressure on you. To have to deal with such a bitch all the time. Or maybe that's why you're barely here.

TIM. I'm barely here because I'm out there working my ass off for *us*.

MALLORY. No, you're running away from us, because you can, but I can't: I'm home alone with nothing to do because I lost my job because I was pregnant with a baby that *died* so you'll forgive me if I'm a little touchy every now and then.

TIM. Look, I know how hard this has been for you—

MALLORY. You don't know! You have no idea. None. Zero.

TIM. Oh I have no idea? I have no idea? I haven't experienced any loss?? Any heartbreaking fucking loss? Is that right, Mallory?

MALLORY. That's right!

TIM. *(Shouting now.)* Well then fuck you!! Just…fuck you.

   His back goes out.

Oh shit.

   Beat.

(Quietly; he's broken up.) It makes me wanna die what's happened. It makes me not believe in God. It makes me lose faith in all the things I used to have faith in.

MALLORY. Like what.

TIM. I don't know. *(Then, very simply.)* That life would turn out okay.

MALLORY. You have a pretty storybook life, Timmy, according to most of the world.

TIM. It would be a big deal never to be a dad.

MALLORY. Then leave me. Leave me and find someone who can give you a kid.

   He turns around, even though it pains him.

TIM. I would never do that.

   Beat.

MALLORY. *(Simply, quietly.)* I'm so lost, Tim.
…I mean, I'm scared for it to work. How crazy is that?

TIM. It's not crazy.

MALLORY. *(As she's walking.)* And I don't know if it would even change anything. Maybe we'd both still be stuck in our own stupid shit.

TIM. Oh we definitely would be.

MALLORY. Then why are we doing this?

TIM. …To have a kid, I guess.

MALLORY. *(Sarcastic, rueful.)* …Well, *that's* a ridiculous reason.

TIM. *(Simply.)* To try to be happy.

MALLORY. You are happy.

TIM. Am I?

MALLORY. I hope so. Because if you aren't, who is.

> *He stands; the lights shift. In this final sequence of the play, the pace should build and build, the lines tight to each other, at times even overlapping, like a song.*

TIM. *(To the audience.)* I once went on a date with this woman who asked if I had to choose, would I pick fame or money. City or countryside, sex or food…those kinds of questions. Then she asked whether I'd pick tennis or my family, and I swear to God I stood up and left. I mean, what kind of question is that? I kept thinking no one would ever be asked to make that choice.

SERGEI. And this is what makes you the gigantic asshole that you are, Tim Porter. Because you do not even *realize* the choice you have made.

MALLORY. *(To the audience, conflicted.)* The in vitro works. It works.

SERGEI. I made same choice, just a child, not knowing the finality of this choice that I was making.

MALLORY. I wake up every morning expecting it to end.

GALINA. *(To the audience.)* After we get engaged, I say, "Sergei, let's call my mother." He says, "But you do not even like your mother, why should we call her right away with our private happy news?" And I think about that. It is not often that Sergei should stump me with a question.

MALLORY. It keeps going.

GALINA. And then he says: "You know, you are lucky. At least you know your mother well enough to dislike her."

MALLORY. I weep at commercials on TV. I weep when I see mothers struggling with their children. I'm enormous; I catch sight of my shadow and have never been more afraid. It's spring and I'm huge; I've just been consuming time.

SERGEI. I serve at love – 2, and I want. I want and I want and I want and I want. There are thousands of people here tonight and if each one represented one of my wants, there would still not be enough.

TIM. How do we get to the bottom of wanting?

SERGEI. I want to justify all the sacrifices. I want to be faithful to my wife. I want to have sex with all the women of the world. I want to die. I want to live. I want to say goodbye to my parents. I never want to say goodbye.

TIM. *(Tortured by all this.)* I want quiet. In my mind. The kind of quiet that can't be interrupted by wanting. I wanna be the kind of dad my dad was.

MALLORY. But then, it's just…happening. I feel the pressure and I feel the pain and I am not in control, but really I never was; already my life is not my own; my body is not my own—which might be what it's like to die, to let go, and I do: I grit my teeth and breathe through my nose and with one enormous whoosh, I push everything else away so I can meet my son.

SERGEI. So what can I do? I picture their faces while I still can and I take each ball, one at a time. This one is a way of saying I miss you. This one is a way of saying I love you. This one is a way of saying why did you never teach me to cook even the simplest thing? This one is a way of saying—fuck you for leaving me! Fuck you for teaching me with your last lesson that we are all alone.

GALINA. But you are not alone! Don't you remember? I said yes. I said, "I love you too." I said, "You are right, we don't need to call my mother right now. You are all I need." I said, "Don't you know there is occasionally daily special? And it is not only made fresh that day, it is good price! And so you have to get it when you see it. You have to buy it and you have to eat it, immediately."

SERGEI. *I* said that!

GALINA. Then do it!!
This is your chance, Sergei. Do it. Now. You are right here; it's right in front of you.

MALLORY. He's here. He sloshed out of me like a gigantic fish. And I was scared but not as much as I expected—of holding him, of being someone's mother—and he stared up at me with these eyes from another world and all that was left was joy.

TIM. But I wasn't there.

MALLORY. It's not possible he's here. And it's also not possible he was ever *not* here.

TIM. I was in the middle of a first-round match at Wimbledon against a not very good eighteen-year-old from Galveston, Texas. I didn't stop when I saw Mallory leave my box, two days from her due date. I kept playing.

MALLORY. You weren't there.

GALINA. You are here, Sergei. And you are alive.

TIM. And I lost. I lost the match anyway.

SERGEI. *(A realization.)* I am alive.

TIM. You asshole, Tim. You loser. You asshole.

MALLORY. It will never be enough, Tim.

TIM. I'm so sorry, Mallory, but I have to play. If I stop, I can't breathe. If I stop, I'll be forgotten. If I stop…I don't know who I am.

MALLORY. *(Firmly but with affection.)* Come on, Tim Porter. You're Mallory Sinclair's husband; that's who you are.

TIM. *(Laughing, all of a sudden.)* Well, that's true. I am that…I am that.

SERGEI. Tim is crouching behind the baseline, laughing or crying— I can't tell which. I'm up 4–2 and moving him around court like dog on leash and somehow he finds this hilarious.

MALLORY. And you're a dad.

TIM. I'm someone's dad.

MALLORY. *(Quietly, simply.)* You can do it, Timmy. And we will love you when you're old. When no one talks about you on TV any-more. When they can't even remember your name.

TIM. *(Turning to the audience.)* And for that moment you don't feel the pressure and the failure and the death and the ambition and the coming up short.

    Then: he serves.

SERGEI. He serves very good game. Close points. We're running everywhere.

TIM. Wild, looping, batshit crazy shots. And some of them go in. Enough of them.

SERGEI. He pulls even with me in the set.

TIM. 4 all.

SERGEI, MALLORY, and GALINA. 4 all.

GALINA. The match is so close, and yet—I feel relaxed. Like a bird flying light on the wind, maybe. Like I have, for moment, escaped who I am. It is the way I will feel when we have children, children who want for nothing and yet are still unhappy, because at this point it will occur to me that everyone is just unhappy. And I start to truly enjoy myself.

MALLORY. Why is it that as soon as a baby is born he doesn't wanna go to sleep? What is it that we know before we know it?

SERGEI. There is, at the bottom of everything, an emptiness. We do what we can to run from this. Tree after tree after tree.

TIM. And then Sergei hits the most beautiful backhand of the match and when I look across the net I see that he's crying. I've never seen anything like it. He's sobbing. And hitting balls past me, left and then right.

GALINA. He's crying. My Sergei. And the way he is playing, I know for certain that he will fulfill his destiny. He plays like he belongs on this court, like it is his, *finally*… Like he deserves it.

SERGEI. For first time EVER, it is like we are dancing *together*— me and Tim Porter.

TIM. Just rhythm. Just a pulse of rhythm.

SERGEI. You go back to basics. / Feet apart, racquet back, contact.

TIM. Feet apart, racquet back, contact. Just like you did when you were ten years old.

SERGEI. I go up 5–4. And you start to feel it. Just a little. Just a glimmer. The light at the end of the tunnel.

TIM. *(Contemplative.)* It is fast and slow all at once.

SERGEI. He serves, and it is the mark of champion that in this circumstance, when pressure is immense, he holds for 5 all.

TIM. See, sometimes it's just about tennis. Just about the body.

SERGEI. I throw the ball up; I see it against the lights, against the night sky; I slam it down. I don't have to look; I know it skids off the line and into the darkness. Unhittable.

TIM. 15 – love. Sergei.

SERGEI. 30 – love. Then 30–15. And I taste it. It is sour and it is sweet and I want it so badly, it hurts.

TIM. I whip one past you. 30 all.

SERGEI. But then I pass you down the line. 40–30.

TIM. I leaked the rumor. Of my own retirement. I think I wanted to see how it would feel. To try it on. Like a hat you know you'll wear one day.

SERGEI. Then it is deuce. / Fucking deuce—

TIM. Fucking deuce—

SERGEI. At 5 all in fifth set. I can't believe it. And yet somehow it is always deuce. One is always tied up, tied together, with the other person, no one ahead or behind.

TIM. Do you know how many matches I've played? This is all I've done. This is what I've done with my life.

SERGEI. Deuce. Always deuce. Another deuce.

TIM. I mean, heck…it's a shame we get old.

SERGEI. Like a whoosh, right past your ear.

TIM. (*A quick stream-of-consciousness.*) "Tim," someone calls out, "Tim"—as if he knows me. And then we are in the middle of the point and my feet are moving and my mind is on overdrive and there are a ton of stars over our heads and it's the middle of the night and it's the middle of my life only it's the end, and my son is already grown, and my parents have been gone many years and I am old; I am no longer a boy.

    A sad realization, and now we slow down.

I am no longer a boy…

I've loved this game, every second. But I've given my son my name, so one day he'll be a man named Tim Porter, just like his dad and his dad's dad. And now I hold him in my arms by the window, a different Timmy than he was even yesterday—this is how quickly he changes; every day he is a *new boy*—and the autumn sun's setting and the sky's full of all these crazy colors and they spread over us like a wreath, like a halo of light. Like the end and the beginning of everything.

> *Tim and Sergei play on, the sounds of the cheering crowd and of the ball being hit reverberating faster and faster as the lights fade.*

End of Play

PROPERTY LIST

(Use this space to create props lists for your production)

59

SOUND EFFECTS
(Use this space to create sound effects lists for your production)

Note on Songs/Recordings, Images, or Other Production Design Elements

Be advised that Dramatists Play Service, Inc., neither holds the rights to nor grants permission to use any songs, recordings, images, or other design elements mentioned in the play. It is the responsibility of the producing theater/organization to obtain permission of the copyright owner(s) for any such use. Additional royalty fees may apply for the right to use copyrighted materials.

For any songs/recordings, images, or other design elements mentioned in the play, works in the public domain may be substituted. It is the producing theater/organization's responsibility to ensure the substituted work is indeed in the public domain. Dramatists Play Service, Inc., cannot advise as to whether or not a song/arrangement/recording, image, or other design element is in the public domain.

NOTES
(Use this space to make notes for your production)

NOTES
(Use this space to make notes for your production)

NOTES
(Use this space to make notes for your production)